D1544623

WITHDRAWN

Fact Finders®
SERIOUSLY TRUE MYSTERIES

THE CASE OF THE

TRAIN WITHOUT WHEELS

and Other
True History
Mysteries
for You to Solve

by Patrice Sherman

Consultant: Dennis Showalter
Professor of History
Colorado College
Colorado Springs, Colorado

CAPSTONE PRESS
a capstone imprint

Fact Finders are published by Capstone Press,
1710 Roe Crest Drive, North Mankato, Minnesota 56003.
www.capstonepub.com

Books published by Capstone Press are manufactured with paper
containing at least 10 percent post-consumer waste.

Library of Congress Cataloging-in-Publication Data
Sherman, Patrice.
The case of the train without wheels and other true history mysteries for you to solve / by Patrice Sherman.
p. cm. —(Fact finders. Seriously true mysteries)
Includes bibliographical references and index.
Summary: "Nonfiction history information is presented as mysteries for readers to solve. With the turn of a page, readers
learn how to solve the true history mystery"—Provided by publisher.
ISBN 978-1-4296-7626-7 (library binding)
1. History—Anecdotes—Juvenile literature. 2. History—Miscellanea—Juvenile literature. I. Title. II. Series.
D10.S525 2012
909—dc23   2011025643

Editorial Credits

Jennifer Besel, editor; Veronica Correia and Tracy Davies McCabe, designers; Wanda Winch, media researcher;
    Laura Manthe, production specialist

Photo Credits

Alamy: Barry Iverson, 6 (bottom right), Classic Image, 20 (top left), Everett Collection Inc, 16 (bottom left), North Wind
Picture Archives, 11, The Art Gallery Collection, 12; AP Images, 27; Corbis: Bettmann, 8 (top) Dreamstime: Jeff Schultes,
23 (bottom); Getty Images: Time Life Pictures/Francis Miller, 26; Library of Congress: Prints and Photographs Division,
10 (top), 18 (top), 20 (bottom left), 21 (middle), 25, Rare Books and Special Collections, 17 (right); National Archives
and Records Administration (NARA): 24 (bottom), cover (middle left), CPhoM. Robert F. Sargent (Coast Guard), 22 (top);
Newscom: DanitaDelimont.com "Danita Delimont Photography"/Kenneth Garrett, 5(middle), SIPA/Alfred, 28 (middle);
Shutterstock: 4ustudio, 13 (back), 14 (back), agorulko, cover (middle right), Andrey Yurlov, 19 (back), 20 (back), c., cover
(bottom left), 9 (bottom right), catrin81, 15, 16, Chengyuan Yang, 5 (back), 6 (back), David W. Leindecker, 18 (bottom),
Dhoxax, 7 (back), 8 (back), EchoArt, 21 (bottom left), Feng Yu, 21 (top right), Fotoline, 5 (back), 6 (back), Hodag Media,
cover (top left), I. Quintanilla, 7 (right), IgorGolovniov, 10 (bottom), Irina Tischenko, 4 (middle), 29 (middle), Janaka
Dhamrasena, 9 (back, top right), 10 (back), Jeff Schultes, 21 (top left), Jeremy Swinborne, cover (top right), Leksele, 19
(bottom left), Matt Trommer, 17 (back), 18 (back), Mirek Hejnicki, cover (middle right), Molodec, 21 (back), 22 (back), NIK,
13 (middle), Rachelle Burnside, cover (bottom right), S_E, 23 (back), 24 (back), Studio 37, 4 (bottom), trekandshoot, cover
(top), Vitaly Korovin, cover (middle), Vladimir Niktin, cover (bottom left), Vladimir Wrangel, 27 (back), 28 (back), wisiel,
cover (bottom), www.JenPicked.com : Jen Machen, 21 (back))

Printed in the United States of America in Brainerd, Minnesota.
102011   006406BANGS12

TABLE OF CONTENTS

DIGGING UP ANSWERS

How did that ancient ruler die? Did that explorer get back home? From ancient mummies to missing travelers, mysteries lurk throughout history. But forget the magnifying glass. A globe and the Internet would be better tools to sleuth out the answers in this book.

BEFORE CONTINUING, PLEASE STATE THE HISTORY DETECTIVE'S PROMISE:

I will read each one-page mystery completely. I will try to solve each mystery to the best of my ability. I will not use this book as scratch paper. I will not peek at the answer on the flip side of the page. Only after I have solved the mystery or worn out my brain trying, may I turn the page.

The calendar's days are numbered. So get solving some of history's mysteries. But proceed with caution. You may experience a loss of time.

Doomed to the Tomb

Spin: -7
Tilt: -16

TESTS FOUND:
- dark spot at the back of skull
- broken leg
- broken and missing ribs
- clubbed foot
- curved spine
- signs of malaria
- signs of bone disease
- signs of infection, possibly from injuries

Name of patient: **Tutankhamun** (also known as **King Tut**)

Job: **pharaoh of Egypt**

Age at time of death: **about 19**

Date of death: **1323 BC**

Date body discovered: **1922**

Location of body: **tomb in Egypt**

Tests performed: **CT Scan, DNA analysis, X-ray**

What was this patient's cause of death?

What Killed the King?

Scientists are close to solving this mystery. They're not 100 percent sure how King Tut died. But many think they have the answer. For years everyone thought King Tut had been murdered. An X-ray done in 1968 showed a dark spot at the back of his skull. Some archaeologists believed the spot was caused by a blow to the head.

In 2005 scientists did a CT scan of Tut's mummy. This scan proved the spot was really two loose skull fragments. The ancient Egyptians used **resins** to preserve bodies. These resins cling to bones. Scientists didn't find any resins on the inner edges of the skull fragments. That meant the skull was broken after death. The edges of the broken leg bones did have resin on them. It is likely that the leg had been broken before death.

In 2010 DNA tests also showed that Tut had malaria. Malaria is a **parasite** that destroys red blood cells. The disease causes weakness and sometimes death.

Here's what scientists think happened. King Tut probably broke his leg. A short time later he came down with malaria. Weakened by injury, Tut could not fight off the disease and died.

King Tut's mummy

resin—a sticky substance that comes from the sap of some trees
parasite—an animal or plant that lives on or inside another animal or plant

LIVING DEAD

It was Giuseppe Fiorelli's dream job. He was leading the search at one of Italy's most amazing historical sites. Workers sifted through layers of fine, rocky soil. They searched for clues about the ancient world that had once been there. Often the workers uncovered strangely shaped holes. The holes contained bits of human or animal bones but nothing else.

For three years Fiorelli puzzled over those holes. They looked empty, but he was sure they held a secret. But how do you save a hole? Finally he had an idea. Fiorelli had his workers fill the holes with plaster. When they removed the ash from around the dried plaster, everyone was shocked. The plaster had molded in the shapes of men, women, and children twisted in pain. These people had died in some horrible tragedy.

What happened?

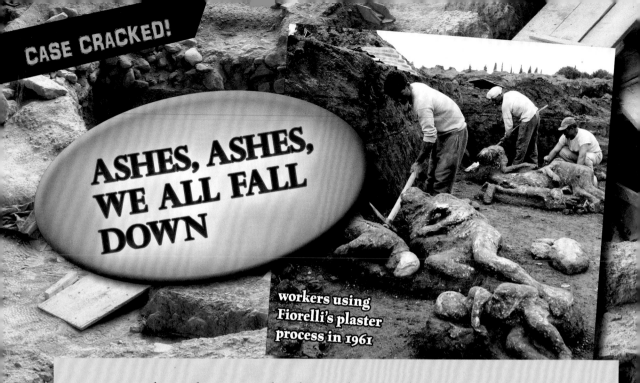

ASHES, ASHES, WE ALL FALL DOWN

workers using Fiorelli's plaster process in 1961

In 1860 the Naples Museum hired **archaeologist** Giuseppe Fiorelli. He was to lead the **excavation** of Pompeii, Italy. Fiorelli realized that the holes in the rock were shaped like people. When he filled the spaces with plaster, he created plaster sculptures of ancient Romans dying. These sculptures showed the powerful impact of a disaster at Pompeii.

Pompeii was located just 1 mile (1.6 kilometers) from the foot of the volcano Mount Vesuvius. About 20,000 people lived in Pompeii. It was a thriving city with wide streets, an outdoor theater, and a swimming pool. In the summer of AD 79, the volcano erupted. Black ash spewed into the sky. Red-hot lava poured down the mountainside. Rocks exploded from the volcano and hurled to the ground like bombs. Pompeii was buried under up to 20 feet (6 meters) of ash.

Thousands of people couldn't escape the volcano's ash and died in the streets. After many years the ash hardened into rock around the bodies. Eventually the bodies rotted away, leaving holes shaped like the victims.

archaeologist—a scientist who studies how people lived in the past
excavation—digging in the earth to search for ancient remains

MYSTERY MAN

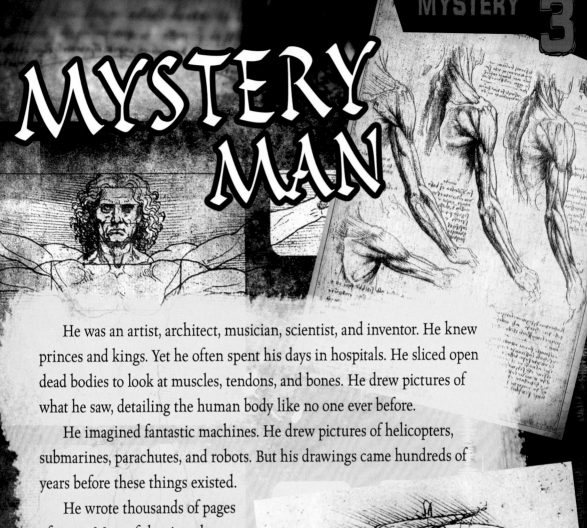

He was an artist, architect, musician, scientist, and inventor. He knew princes and kings. Yet he often spent his days in hospitals. He sliced open dead bodies to look at muscles, tendons, and bones. He drew pictures of what he saw, detailing the human body like no one ever before.

He imagined fantastic machines. He drew pictures of helicopters, submarines, parachutes, and robots. But his drawings came hundreds of years before these things existed.

He wrote thousands of pages of notes. Most of the time, he wrote the words in mirror-image from right to left.

He also painted a portrait of a smiling lady. People say her eyes seem to look at you no matter where you stand in the room.

WHO WAS THIS MAN?

ITALIAN GENIUS

Leonardo da Vinci

Our mystery man was born near Florence, Italy, in 1452. He was one of the world's greatest artists and inventors. He also excelled at music, engineering, biology, math, astronomy, and mapmaking. He even found time to investigate fireworks. Who was he?

This great scientist and artist was Leonardo da Vinci. Leonardo excelled in many areas. He kept careful notes of his ideas and observations in notebooks. His writing in the books is often strange. Leonardo usually wrote from right to left with his left hand. The letters are backward and are best read using a mirror.

Leonardo's most famous painting is the *Mona Lisa*. This portrait of a woman hangs in the Louvre Museum in Paris, France. People travel from all over the world to see her celebrated smile.

Mona Lisa

SURPRISE PARTY

On December 16, 1773, 16-year-old Samuel Cooper attended a very unusual party. Invitation came by word of mouth only. Around 7:00 that evening, Cooper joined a group of men wearing face paint and feathers. They crept silently through the streets to the city's dock. The men boarded the ships. "No noise was heard," Cooper wrote afterward, "except the occasional clink of the hatchet in opening the boxes ..."

By 10:00 the party was over. The men left as quickly as they had come. The only evidence they left behind was a brown mess floating in the harbor.

WHAT KIND OF PARTY WAS THIS?

FIGHTING TAXES

In the 1700s Great Britain ruled the 13 American colonies. The British **Parliament** set laws and created taxes. But colonists weren't allowed to vote for the people in Parliament. Over time the colonists became increasingly angry because they didn't have a voice in their government.

By 1773 Parliament had canceled most of its taxes because of the colonists' violent **protests**. But one tax remained. There was still a tax on tea, a favorite drink in the colonies. In a tricky move, Parliament lowered the tax on tea that came from Britain. Tea from other places carried a higher tax. Parliament thought colonists would pay the lower tax on British tea. Many colonists disagreed.

In Boston a group of colonists called the Sons of Liberty planned a protest. On the night of December 16, 1773, more than 100 men boarded three British tea ships. They dumped 342 crates of tea into Boston Harbor.

The protest made Parliament and the British king furious. They sent soldiers into Boston and closed the city's ports. Anger boiled over on both sides. And on April 19, 1775, the first shots of the Revolutionary War were fired.

The 1773 event was the Boston Tea Party. It wasn't really a party. It was a protest that helped lead America to fight for independence.

Parliament—a group of people who make laws and run the government in some countries
protest—to object to something strongly and publicly

THE QUOTATION FROM SAMUEL COOPER ON PAGE 11 WAS TAKEN FROM HIS WRITTEN ACCOUNT OF THE BOSTON TEA PARTY, MADE AVAILABLE BY THE BOSTON TEA PARTY HISTORICAL SOCIETY WEB SITE. COOPER WAS A MEMBER OF THE SONS OF LIBERTY. HE ALSO FOUGHT IN THE BATTLES OF LEXINGTON-CONCORD, BUNKER HILL, AND MANY OTHERS.

Into the Wild

April 29, 1805

Set out this morning at the usual hour; the wind was moderate; I walked on shore with one man. About 8 A. M. we fell in with two brown or yellow bear; both of which we wounded; one of them made his escape, the other after my firing on him pursued me seventy or eighty yards, but fortunately had been so badly wounded that he was unable to pursue so closely as to prevent my charging my gun; we again repeated our fir and killed him.

It was a male not fully grown, we estimated his weight at 300 lbs, not having the means of ascertaining it precisely ... Its color is yellowish brown, the eyes small, black, and piercing; the front of the fore legs near the feet is usually black; the fur is finer, thicker, and deeper than that of the black bear.

November 16, 1805

This was a clear morning and the wind pretty high. We could see the waves, like small mountains, rolling out in the ocean, and pretty bad in the bay.

We are now at the end of our voyage, which has been completely accomplished according to the intention of the expedition, the object of which was to discover a passage by the way of the Missouri and Columbia rivers to the Pacific Ocean.

WHO WROTE THESE JOURNALS, AND WHAT WERE THESE PEOPLE DOING?

Journal Journey

In 1804 President Thomas Jefferson asked a group of 33 men to go on an **expedition**. The western half of the United States was unsettled by white people. Jefferson wanted to know what the area contained.

The Corps of Discovery traveled more than 8,000 miles (12,875 km). The men met 48 American Indian tribes and drew 140 maps. Many of the men wrote in journals about the wildlife they saw. Their journals described more than 200 species of plants and animals that had been unknown to them before.

The journal entry from April 29 belonged to Meriwether Lewis. Lewis was co-leader of the Corps of Discovery together with William Clark. His entry describes a dangerous meeting with a grizzly bear. Sergeant Patrick Gass wrote the November 16 entry. In all, the men of the Lewis and Clark expedition wrote almost 5,000 pages. The journals tell of what they found west of the Mississippi River.

> **expedition**—a journey with a goal such as exploring or searching for something

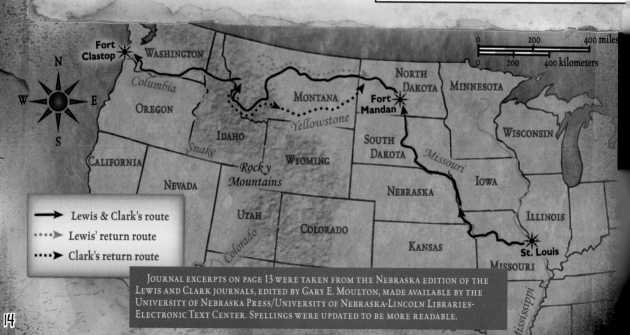

Lewis & Clark's route

Lewis' return route

Clark's return route

INVISIBLE TRAIN

The Underground Train,
Strange as it seems,
Carried many passengers
And never was seen

It wasn't made of wood,
It wasn't made of steel;
A man-made train that
Ran without wheels.

The train was known
By many a name.
But the greatest of all
Was "The Freedom Train"

WAS THERE REALLY A
TRAIN WITHOUT WHEELS?

SAVING SLAVES

Before the Civil War (1861–1865), almost all African-Americans in the southern United States were slaves. Slaves had to do whatever their masters commanded. If they disobeyed, they were whipped, branded, or even killed. By 1804 most northern states had abolished slavery. Many slaves slipped away, attempting to find freedom in the north.

The train without wheels wasn't a train. It was the Underground Railroad, a system of people and places that helped slaves escape.

From about 1830 to 1861, the Underground Railroad helped thousands of slaves. Slaves didn't travel by train underground, though. "Underground" meant the system was secret. "Railroad" stood for the hiding spots slaves stopped at along the way. People who helped slaves travel north were called conductors. No one knows exactly how many slaves conductors helped. Levi and Catharine Coffin helped more than 2,000 slaves. Former slave Harriet Tubman led about 300 slaves to freedom.

People in southern states were angry that northern people supported the Underground Railroad. The fight over slavery divided the United States. The fight led to the Civil War. Near the end of the war, the U.S. government passed the 13th Amendment to the Constitution. This change made slavery illegal in all states.

Song lyrics on page 15 are taken from "The Ballad of the Underground Railroad" written by historian Charles L. Blockson and James McGowan. The song was printed in Blockson's book *The Underground Railroad in Pennsylvania* published by Flame International in 1981.

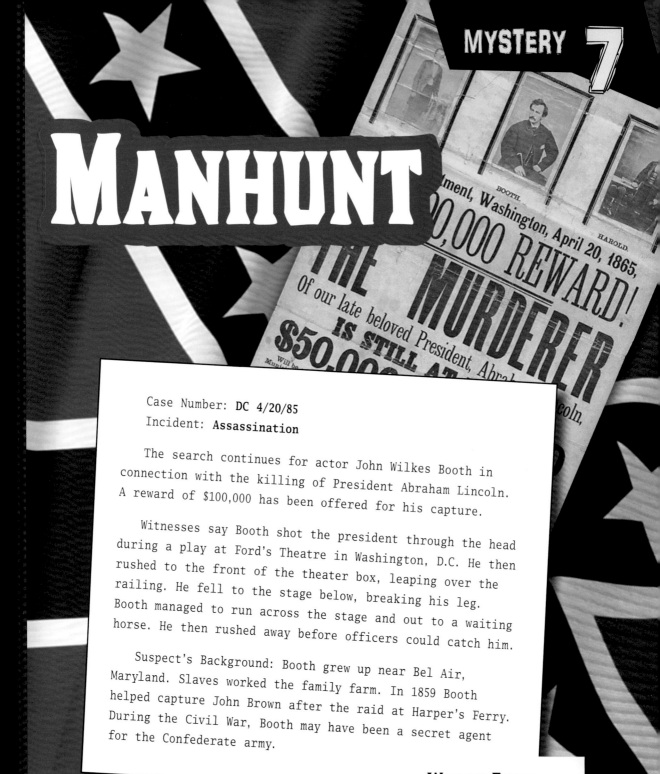

MANHUNT

THE MURDERER

Of our late beloved President, Abraham...

IS STILL AT...

$50,00...

ment, Washington, April 20, 1865,

00,000 REWARD!

BOOTH.

HAROLD.

coln,

Case Number: **DC 4/20/85**
Incident: **Assassination**

The search continues for actor John Wilkes Booth in connection with the killing of President Abraham Lincoln. A reward of $100,000 has been offered for his capture.

Witnesses say Booth shot the president through the head during a play at Ford's Theatre in Washington, D.C. He then rushed to the front of the theater box, leaping over the railing. He fell to the stage below, breaking his leg. Booth managed to run across the stage and out to a waiting horse. He then rushed away before officers could catch him.

Suspect's Background: Booth grew up near Bel Air, Maryland. Slaves worked the family farm. In 1859 Booth helped capture John Brown after the raid at Harper's Ferry. During the Civil War, Booth may have been a secret agent for the Confederate army.

WHY DID BOOTH KILL THE PRESIDENT?

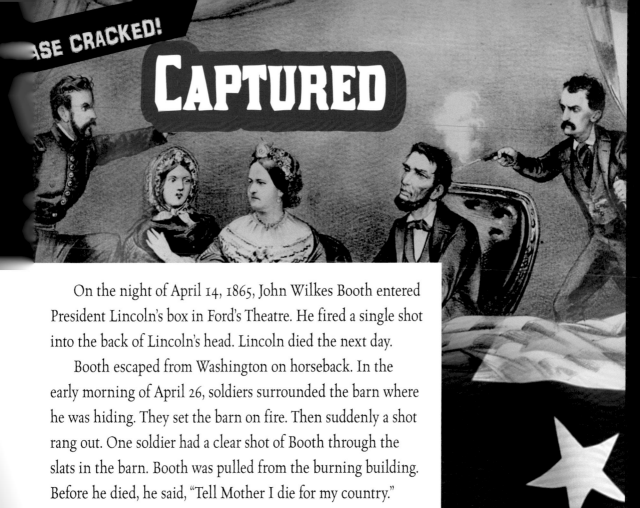

CAPTURED

On the night of April 14, 1865, John Wilkes Booth entered President Lincoln's box in Ford's Theatre. He fired a single shot into the back of Lincoln's head. Lincoln died the next day.

Booth escaped from Washington on horseback. In the early morning of April 26, soldiers surrounded the barn where he was hiding. They set the barn on fire. Then suddenly a shot rang out. One soldier had a clear shot of Booth through the slats in the barn. Booth was pulled from the burning building. Before he died, he said, "Tell Mother I die for my country."

The United States was divided over slavery during the Civil War. During the war southern states left the union and formed their own government. They called themselves the Confederate States of America. Booth was a strong supporter of the Confederacy. In fact, when he said he died for his country, he was talking about the Confederacy. Booth believed that African-Americans should not have freedoms like white people. He killed the president because he disagreed with the decision to give slaves freedom and rights.

Wicked Race

It was the year 1910. Two explorers set out to achieve what no one had done before. They both wanted to be the first to reach the South Pole. The race was on. Two men, two different plans.

	ROALD AMUNDSEN	ROBERT FALCON SCOTT
EXPERIENCE	A seasoned explorer, Amundsen had spent a winter in Antarctica when his ship froze into the ice.	A naval officer, Scott tried and failed to reach the South Pole 10 years before.
CREW	Four men left base camp with Amundsen on the trip to the pole.	Sixteen men left base camp with Scott. Four were later chosen to go all the way to the pole with him.
TRANSPORTATION ON THE ICE	52 sled dogs pulling four sleds	two motor sledges, 10 ponies, 23 sled dogs, 13 sleds
SUPPLIES	four months of supplies for five men	supplies for the 16 men who traveled part of the way; supplies for four men to travel to the pole
DATE LEFT BASE CAMP	October 19, 1911	November 1, 1911

ONLY ONE COULD WIN.
WHO WOULD IT BE?

Winners and Losers

BOTH MEN MADE IT TO THE SOUTH POLE. BUT WHO GOT THERE FIRST?

Roald Amundsen

Robert Falcon Scott

Roald Amundsen won. He left base camp two weeks before Scott. He traveled with fewer men and had sled dogs to pull the loads. He also started 60 nautical miles (111 km) closer to the pole. Amundsen reached the pole on December 14, 1911. He and his men retuned safely to base camp on January 25, 1912.

Robert Falcon Scott reached the pole on January 17, 1912. He lost the race due to earlier decisions. Almost 170 nautical miles (315 km) from the pole, Scott chose four men to go to the pole with him. But he had only enough food for three others. Transportation became a problem too. The ponies froze to death, and the motor sledges broke down. The sled dogs had been sent back to base camp. The men had to pull the sleds themselves. They quickly became starved and exhausted.

Scott and his men died on the way back. Scott wrote in a letter before he died, "I do not regret this journey ... Had we lived, I should have had a tale to tell of the hardihood, endurance, and courage of my companions. [But] ... These rough notes and our dead bodies must tell the tale ... "

On the Beach

Omaha Beach, June 6, 1944

Omaha, Nebraska, is nowhere near the ocean.

Where was this beach, and what was the man doing there?

Fighting in France

By 1944 World War II had been raging for nearly five years. Germany's **dictator** Adolf Hitler and his Nazi soldiers had taken control of most of Western Europe. The **Allied forces** were fighting Germany. On June 6, 1944, 160,000 Allied soldiers invaded France at Normandy Beach. They had come to free France from Germany.

The invasion of Normandy Beach was called D-Day. The Allies divided the beach into five sections. Each section was given a code name—Omaha, Utah, Gold, Juno, and Sword. Omaha Beach saw some of the fiercest fighting. Under steady gunfire from the Germans, Allied soldiers took control of the beach. After a day of heavy combat, German forces retreated. During the summer of 1944, Allied troops continued to push German troops eastward. Less than a year later, Nazi Germany surrendered.

The mystery is solved. Omaha Beach was the code name for a section of Normandy Beach in France. The man in the picture was one of thousands of Allied soldiers who had come to fight the Nazis.

dictator—someone who has complete control of a country, often ruling it unjustly
Allied forces—countries united against Germany during World War II, including France, the United States, Canada, Great Britain, and others

SECRET MESSAGES

On February 23, 1945, U.S. military commanders in the Pacific region received a radio transmission. The message was from Marines on the Japanese island Iwo Jima. Four days earlier, the Marines had launched an attack on the island. Fighting between U.S. and Japanese forces was intense. The Marines needed to take control of Iwo Jima if the United States was to win the war. The soldiers cheered when they read the message.

Dibeh, Shi-Da, Dah-Nes-Tsa, Tkin, Shush, Wol-La-Chee, Moasi, Lin, Yeh-hes.

Translated into English it read, "Sheep, Uncle, Ram, Ice, Bear, Ant, Cat, Horse, Itch."

WHAT DID THE MESSAGE MEAN?

WALKING CODE

The United States entered World War II in 1941. Soldiers sent secret information to each other in coded messages. But the Japanese quickly broke all the codes. The U.S. military needed an unbreakable code. The American Indian language of Navajo was exactly what they needed. Navajo is one of the most difficult languages to learn. Much of its meaning depends on tone and pitch.

During the war more than 400 Navajo men served as "code talkers." One code talker would send a message by radio to a fellow code talker. The talker who received the message translated it into English. Then he gave it to his commander.

The Navajo words were used a couple of different ways. Sometimes the first letter of each word in the English translation spelled out the message. Other times code talkers used entire Navajo words for military terms.

The message from Iwo Jima used the first letter of the translation method.

Sheep **U**ncle **R**am **I**ce **B**ear **A**nt **C**at **H**orse **I**tch

The letters spell out Suribachi. Mount Suribachi is the highest point on Iwo Jima. It meant that the United States controlled the island, and Japan had lost a key battle in the war.

Navajo code talkers

Navajo Word in English	Navajo Pronunciation	Code Meaning
black sheep	DEBEH-LI-ZINI	squad
short raccoon	HA-A-SID-AL-SIZI-GIH	scout
tortoise	CHAY-DA-GAHI	tank
iron fish	BESH-LO	submarine
potatoes	NI-MA-SI	grenade

Longest Walk

"The crowd moved in closer and then began to follow me, calling me names," Elizabeth Eckford later recalled about this moment. "I still wasn't afraid. Just a little bit nervous. Then my knees started to shake all of a sudden and I wondered whether I could make it to the center entrance a block away. It was the longest block I ever walked in my whole life."

Who was Elizabeth Eckford, and why was the crowd so angry with her?

Equal Rights

In the 1950s black and white people in the southern United States were **segregated**. Blacks couldn't sit next to whites on buses or eat in the same restaurants. Black and white children could not attend the same schools. African-Americans wanted to be treated the same as white people. In 1954 the U.S. Supreme Court ruled that schools could no longer be divided by race.

On September 4, 1957, Eckford arrived at Central High in Little Rock, Arkansas. A mob of white people surrounded her. People cursed, spat, and threatened to kill her. Eckford tried to enter the school. National Guard soldiers, on orders from the governor, blocked her way. On September 25 President Dwight Eisenhower sent the U.S. Army to Little Rock. With the army to protect her, Eckford was finally allowed to go to school.

Elizabeth Eckford was trying to desegregate Central High. The mob screaming at her was angry that blacks and whites would go to school together.

Eckford wasn't the only African-American student who tried to go to Central High that day. Eight other students had been chosen to go to school there. They too were denied access to the school before the army arrived.

The Little Rock Nine, as the students were called, became heroes of the Civil Rights Movement. Seeing children walk past angry mobs made people think about the affects of segregation.

segregate—to keep people of different races apart in schools and other public places

ECKFORD'S QUOTATION ON PAGE 25 WAS TAKEN FROM *THE LONG SHADOW OF LITTLE ROCK* BY DAISY BATES PUBLISHED BY THE UNIVERSITY OF ARKANSAS PRESS IN 1986.

POLITICAL BIRDS

In 1961 a wall was built. It wasn't the longest wall in the world, but it was probably the most hated. The concrete and wire structure wound 103 miles (166 km) around half of this German city. It stood 12 to 15 feet (3.7 to 4.6 m) high and was up to 4 feet (1.2 m) thick. It separated neighbors, friends, and families.

Then one night, years later, the woodpeckers showed up on the western side. They started chipping away at the cement wall. These woodpeckers didn't have feathers. They had hammers, chisels, and iron pipes.

WHO WERE THESE WOODPECKERS?

WALL BREAKERS

After World War II, Germany was divided into two countries. East Germany was controlled by a dictatorship in Soviet Russia. West Germany had a democracy. People weren't allowed to move freely between the two countries.

The city of Berlin was located in East Germany. Half of it, however, belonged to West Germany. Millions of East Germans went to Berlin to try to escape. In 1961 the East German government built a wall around West Berlin. Guards were ordered to shoot anyone attempting to climb the wall.

By the late 1980s Soviet Russia had lost much of its power. On November 9, 1989, the East German government finally allowed people to travel freely between East and West Germany. Germans on both sides celebrated in the streets.

The night of November 9, hundreds of West Germans began to chip away at the wall. They worked with sledgehammers and chisels. People called them the *mauerspechte*, German for "wall woodpeckers." By July 1990 the wall was completely destroyed. Germany became a single nation again on October 3, 1990.

HISTORY'S
MYSTERIES

Here's one last mystery. What do the clues describe?

1) It affects our lives today.

2) It adds to our knowledge of the world.

3) It inspires people to stand up for their rights.

4) It helps us avoid mistakes.

THE CLUES DESCRIBE HISTORY!

Everything in our world is shaped by history.
Explorers have added to our knowledge of the world.
Artists let us see it in new ways. Wars helped create
some nations and end others. Ordinary people stand
up for their rights and change society.

Historians are like detectives. They're always on
the trail of a mystery, searching for clues. If you love
mysteries too, then digging into history just might
be a dream come true!

GLOSSARY

Allied forces (AL-lyd FOR-seyz)—countries united against Germany during World War II (1939–1945), including France, the United States, Canada, Great Britain, and others

archaeologist (ar-kee-AH-luh-jist)—a scientist who studies how people lived in the past

dictator (DIK-tay-tuhr)—someone who has complete control of a country, often ruling it unjustly

excavation (ek-skuh-VAY-shuhn)—digging in the earth to search for ancient remains

expedition (ek-spuh-DI-shuhn)—a journey with a goal, such as exploring or searching for something

parasite (PAIR-uh-site)—an animal or plant that lives on or inside another animal or plant

Parliament (PAR-luh-muhnt)—a group of people who make laws and run the government in some countries

protest (pro-TEST)—to object to something strongly and publicly

resin (REZ-in)—a yellow or brown, sticky substance that comes from the sap of some trees

segregate (SEG-ruh-gate)—to keep people of different races apart in schools and other public places

READ MORE

Ganeri, Anita. *On Expedition with Lewis and Clark.* Crabtree Connections. New York: Crabtree Pub., 2011.

Llanas, Sheila Griffin. *Who Reached the South Pole First?* Race for History. Mankato, Minn.: Capstone Press, 2011.

Rooney, Anne. *The Berlin Wall.* A Place in History. Mankato, Minn.: Arcturus Pub., 2011.

Samuel, Charlie. *Solving the Mysteries of Pompeii.* Digging into History. New York: Marshall Cavendish Benchmark, 2009.

INTERNET SITES

FactHound offers a safe, fun way to find Internet sites related to this book. All of the sites on FactHound have been researched by our staff.

Here's all you do:

Visit *www.facthound.com*

Type in this code: 9781429676267

 Check out projects, games and lots more at
www.capstonekids.com

INDEX